Labradoodles

A Pet Labradoodle Care Guide

Labradoodles General Info, Purchasing, Care, Cost, Keeping, Health, Supplies, Food, Breeding and More Included!

By Lolly Brown

Copyrights and Trademarks

Disclaimer and Legal Notice

Foreword

Labradoodles became massively popular around the world because of their loving, affectionate and loyal personalities. One of the most unique characteristic of these dogs is their low – shedding qualities. Many Labradoodle hybrids like the toy poodles are relatively smaller for its mature size, which is why even if they reached their maturity, they still look like juvenile or young dogs, sometimes some breeds can get very big just that of a pure bred Labrador's size but the best part is that they maintain that youthful vibe even if they've reached adulthood.

Find out more about this dog breed by delving deeper into its biological information. See if the Labradoodle is the right companion for you and your family by gaining knowledge about its temperament and behavior, the cost it entails in keeping one, its health condition, its major pros and cons as well as how to feed them, groom them, and care for their overall well - being.

Table of Contents

Introduction

The Labradoodle or sometimes known as the "Goldendoodle" are the most outrageously friendly dog breeds out there. They are designer dogs that are a crossbreed of a Labrador and a Poodle. They possess either a relatively small size body or a larger type (depends on the characteristics that they've inherited from their parents) and they can be distinguished because of their curly fur and super carefree personality. In fact, these dogs are so friendly that sometimes their owners have trouble of handling them. This is perhaps a fair warning for those of you who wanted to get a Labradoodle but aren't open to having a very active dog around. When you get this kind of dog, don't expect that it's just going to be like buying a plant!

All Labradoodle types of dog – mini and large – possess one common trait: they have high energy levels! They defy the word "active" because you just can't settle these pet down even if you properly trained them (of course, you can still instill discipline but it doesn't mean that they're just going to sit around and strictly follow your commands), they're just built that way.

Having an active dog like a Labradoodle also means that their diets matter since they burn lots of energies every day, they also need lots of exercise, and they are huge huggers! They will jump right in front of you and at people! It's their way of saying hello or greeting everyone else because they're just really friendly pets. As a matter of fact, socialization is perhaps your least concern compared to other dog breeds because these dogs are a natural when it comes to dealing with people and even other household pets (although smaller ones might be a bad idea – your cat could be crushed!).

Training and handling is probably the biggest concern that you need to take note of if you're going to acquire this type of dog; their super active behaviors can sometimes be a problem if they're not properly trained at an early age. It's just like in us humans, having all that enthusiasm, drive and unwavering passion is good but if there's no discipline and a sense of focus, all that energy can become a problem. So make sure that when you get a

Labradoodle puppy, start teaching them "the basics." You want to teach them how to sit or settle down so that they can be petted by people since these dogs are always craving for attention and affection. Labradoodles are delightful companions that will surely delay you in leaving your house in the morning, and a dog that will make you excited to come back home every night!

Chapter One: Labradoodles Inside Out!

Labradoodles are irresistibly fun and it's the kind of dog that will go out of its way just to please you and get your attention! If you are adventurous, someone who likes to have fun and also a caring person, then this pet could be for you! In this chapter you will receive an introduction to the breed including some basic biological facts and physical characteristics, lifespan as well as the history of how it was originally developed. This chapter will give you background information about these pets. You can also find relevant information under the quick facts section of this chapter, are you ready to let this Labradoodles (literally) rock your world? You asked for it!

Origin and History

These cute furry and fun dogs are created in Australia around the 1980 by a dog veterinarian – no wonder why this dog breed is awesome! But he actually did this on purpose because this vet knows somebody who needed a guide dog but the problem is that his friend was allergic to a dog's coat. This led him to mixing an intelligent dog which is a Labrador retriever and an active low – shedding dog called a Poodle. The result is a service dog that is perfect for someone who has allergies. But contrary to popular belief, these dogs are not totally "hypoallergenic" because no dog is hypoallergenic; labradoodles are just a better choice for those who are suffering from allergic reaction because these breed often secrete less dander than other breed types.

Today, this designer dog is at the verge of becoming its own breed because if one cross bred a labradoodle with another labradoodle, their litters can maintain the physical characteristics that their parents possess.

Unfortunately, since Labradoodles aren't purebred dogs, they are not yet recognized by dog registries and organizations like the American Kennel Club (AKC) as well as countries in Europe and Australia. They are still on the process of getting officially recognized but more work needs to be done in the part of the breeders so that these designer dogs can adhere to the standards. Nevertheless, they are one of the world's must - have pups and they are pretty much the pioneer of cross breeding. Most of their owners are Hollywood celebrities, politicians, sports figures and other notable personalities. They surely captured the hearts of many children and families with their fun loving personalities.

Size, Life Span, and Physical Appearance

Labradoodles have broad heads, their eyebrows are usually well – defined, have dropped ears that are long and furry which is well set, and they are available in many colors. Their coats can sometimes be quite a surprise because since they are a cross, you just don't know what kind of coat you're going to get. It can range from having a straight hair, fleece (wavy) and wool (curly and most allergy friendly of all the Labradoodle coat types). This breed appears to be attractive, bulky, but still graceful. They also appear in different colors such as apricot, chalk (white), black, caramel, red, café, silver, chocolate, cream, parchment, gold as well as blue which make them more adorable!

They mostly differ in size and look and because of that, they are classified into three different sizes. This is the result of the parents that are being mated which gives out various litter puppies. Over time they were able to identify the three different sizes of this breed; the Standard labradoodles stands about 21 – 23 inches for female and 22 – 24 inches for male and weighs 55 – 60 pounds. Medium-sized labradoodles are ideally 17 – 19 inches for female and 19 – 20 inches for male in height and weighs 30 – 40 pounds while smaller labradoodles are 14 -16 inches for both female and male and weighs 16 – 25 pounds. These standards were established by the Tegan Park and Rutland Manor Breeding and Research Centers of Australia and were later on adopted by the Australian Labradoodle Club of America.

Labradoodles are quite versatile dogs which mean that they can live in small or big spaces; however they're not suited for owners that are living in apartments because even if you walk them around the park every day, they still won't be satisfied. These dogs need an outlet, they need to be able to run around the house, and have plenty of activities to do which is why a simple walk in the park won't just cut it.

The major downside of owning a labradoodle is that these dogs often times develop health problems since it's very common among designer breeds. Hip dysplasia is the number one health problem among labradoodles as well as other genetic illnesses like eye problems. This breed has an average lifespan of about 12 - 14 years. If you want a long – term companion (and commitment), then Labradoodles can be a great choice!

Quick Facts

Origin: Australia

Pedigree: crossbreed of Labrador retriever and Poodle

Breed Size: small/large, toy/designer breed

Body Type and Appearance: These dogs have broad heads, their eyebrows are usually well – defined, have dropped ears that are long, well - set and furry, and they are available in many colors.

Height: Standard Labradoodles are 21 – 23 inches for female and 22 – 24 inches for male; Medium-sized Labradoodles are ideally 17 – 19 inches for female and 19 – 20 inches for male; Miniature Labradoodles are 14 -16 inches for female and male

Weight: Standard Labradoodle weighs about 55 – 60 pounds; Medium Labradoodle weighs about 30 – 40 pounds; Miniature – size Labradoodle weighs about 16 – 25 pounds

Coat Length: 4 – 6 inches of loose curls to straight

Coat Texture: Hair, Wool, Fleece

Color: Apricot, Chalk (white), Black, Caramel, Red, Café, Silver, Chocolate, Cream, Parchment, Gold, Blue

Ears: dropped ears, long

Tail: short to medium-length

Temperament: sociable, friendly, trainable, obedient, joyful

Strangers: friendly, with little barking tendencies when properly trained

Other Dogs: generally goes well with other dogs if properly trained and socialized

Other Pets: friendly with other pets

Training: intelligent and easily trained

Exercise Needs: regular amount of exercise but not excessive because they are athletic dogs.

Health Conditions: maybe prone to hereditary genetic diseases. They are prone to eye problems, hip problems such as Hip Dysplasia, coat problems, and genetic eye problems.

Lifespan: average 12 – 14 years

Chapter Two: Labradoodles as Pets

Labradoodles are not just efficient in being guide dogs; they are very affectionate as well. Labradoodles are very much adaptable to their environment (though apartments are not ideal) which makes the extremely friendly to their owner and others around them, and because they are extremely friendly, they are also safe around kids. In this chapter, you will get a whole lot of information about the pros and cons of this breed, some legal requirements you need to follow before keeping one, how they deal with other pets, its personalities and behaviors, and what makes it a great pet. The average costs for each items is also found in this chapter so that you can also be financially prepared.

Is the Labradoodle the Right Pet for You?

These darling and devoted pets get their biggest thrill just by being with their owners. So if you're thinking about welcoming a new family member like the labradoodle, you better get to know what they're going to be like! This section will delve deeper on what makes them great family pets that everyone adores.

Temperament and Behavioral Characteristics

Labradoodles are blessed with outstanding qualities that they got from their parent breeds these dogs are naturally intuitive and can be easily trained. They also love to socialize and a very devoted pet. They love stimulation and attention from their owners, the require companionship and have pretty much proven themselves over the last few decades that they are great family dogs and a true man's best friend.

And because these dogs are continuously sweeping the nation and the entire world for many years, they were recently added to the Oxford English Dictionary, making the word "Labradoodle" a winning word placement for Scrabble players.

You can expect Labradoodles to be around when you are relaxing at the comfort of your home, sure they are very active pets but they also possess a degree of demeanor. And because of their energy level, they can easily adapt and go along well with their owners, kids and other dogs. In fact, they are also good around cats and other household pets. This breed is a good pick if you have cats in the house because they are friendly towards them.

Behavioral Characteristics with other Pets

Labradoodles require a lot of time and attention when it comes to training which is why it could be hard for you to train a lot of Labradoodles, especially if you are a newbie. This kind of breed may not be an easy breed for first time dog owners in terms of handling them.

Owning more than one of any breed is still up to the pet owner since it takes a significant amount of effort in giving them all their needs. Of course, these needs do not only mean that you will provide for their physical daily needs, but also the significant time and affection that is vital for their growth and development. You must be willing to give your best effort in all the aspects of your life when you decide to get a dog.

Pros and Cons of Labradoodle

One of the major advantages of keeping a Labradoodle is their easy to care coats you won't have any problem in terms of grooming them, and it can help you save on grooming expenses as well. Their coats are easy to brush and it doesn't need regular brushing. As mentioned earlier, they are "hypoallergenic" dogs which are another advantage for people who have allergies.

They generally gets along with other dogs or pets as long as they are properly socialized and introduced, and even if they're not you can be rest assured that your Labradoodles will get along with them just fine. They can also be good but quite active lap dogs; they'll constantly kiss you, lick you and move around you! These dogs are highly trainable and they also make a good watch dog. They are agile, very smart, and very active which is why kids love them. They're a fun – loving family companion that will love you and care for you for quite a long time!

When it comes to the disadvantages, Labradoodles may not be suitable for people living in tight – space apartments because they needs lots of exercise and a space to play. They tend to be a bit destructive when bored and if you're leaving in a small house, then you must not leave them alone because for sure your home will get thrashed.

Their naturally active and curious attitude can sometimes lead to trouble if they're not properly trained. They don't do well in isolation, can be quite hard to handle or train and they could also be costly for your family budget.

If you want to sign them up for a kennel show, they may not be allowed since the breed is not yet officially recognized by several major dog registries. You can however sign them up for dog competitions like dog racing or some kind of trick contests but maybe not for showing or the 'pageants of dogs.'

Dog Licensing

Acquiring a license for your pets can be different depending on the country, state and region that you are in. There are certain regulations and restrictions that should be taken in to consideration when purchasing a dog, or in this case a Labradoodle. In the United States, there is no federal requirement for getting a license for your pets, but it is the state that regulates these kinds of rules. Though it is not required for you dogs to get a license, it is important that you do so. It will not just provide a protection for your pet, but also to you as a pet owner. An identification number is placed in your dog licensed which is directly linked to your contact details as the owner. This can be very helpful in case your pet gets lost, it's also called micro-chipping.

It is also important to take note that before you can get your dog a license, you must be vaccinated against rabies. This is the only requirement for you to acquire a license. Dog license are renewable every year which means that you have to get another rabies vaccination.

When you acquire a license for your dog you will be given a dog number that can then be linked to your contact information. If your dog gets lost and someone finds it, its license can be used to track you down so that they'll be able to return your pet to you. You can either use a dog tag (traditional ID collar) or have the option of micro – chipping your pet. Micro – chipping is a procedure in which vets will embed a chip on your dog's skin that contains contact details of the owner, and ultimately serves as a tracker for whoever will find your lost pet.

It is also recommended that your pet should acquire a license or be micro-chip even at an early age or while they are still puppies to be prepared if in case they leave the house without your supervision, during natural disasters, or if he/she accidentally access the doors, gates, or windows. This dog breed is smart and has a very short attention span, they can easily ran off if they see something that will caught their eye without you knowing.

If you want to apply for a dog license, you can search the website of your municipal or state government online. You will be able to download the application form, and just follow the procedure. After filling up the form, you can mail it to their office together with a fee. Although, in some states there is currently no fee for a dog license so make sure to check first and find out how much it cost.

Documentary requirements must be submitted before permanently getting a pet license such as current rabies certificate, spay and neuter proof, and microchip. In most states, these are the main documents needed to get a dog license, although, there might be additional requirements that need to be submitted in other states. The temporary license will be considered only as temporary until you have provided all the necessary requirements.

Other Dog Permits

Licensing requirements for dogs is needed if you want to bring them along with you during your travels domestically or internationally. You may need to get a special permit if you plan to travel with your dog into or out of the country. In some countries, pets are subjected to a quarantine period to make sure that your dog isn't carrying a disease like rabies or other virus. It's also recommended that you bring proper documents such as your state permit for your dog, rabies or vaccinations certificate, and a vet's approval or certificate that the dog or pet is in good health condition; to ensure that there'll be no transfer of virus or diseases to the country you wish to go to with your pet.

Aside from that, there could be other requirements so be sure to check first the country laws regarding bringing of pets or travelling with them in other nations.

Costs of Owning a Dog

Your potential dog will cost a lot more than just purchasing them because you need to feed them, groom them, buy accessories and toys for them, create an adequate environment, care for them when they're sick, acquire license or permits, and pretty much care for their overall needs. If you're not ready for a new set of dog bills, then maybe it's not yet times to acquire a dog breed for that matter. These costs will add up to your daily/monthly budget, it's really like adding a new member of the family.

Aside from that, you also have to keep in mind that these pet expenses will go on for a long time since a dog's average lifespan is up to fifteen years. Not only that, when your dog dies one day, it will also cost you money.

Below is an overview of the major things you need to spend on for your Labradoodle check out the following:

- **Purchase Price of Labradoodle:** average labradoodle puppies cost $500, sometimes it can cost up to $1,500 - $1,500. There are breeders who would require you to give an initial deposit when purchasing one but before you do, make sure to get a Labradoodle on trusted and reputable dog breeders.

- **Food/Treats:** The cost of a high quality diet still depends on the brand. For your dog to keep the healthy and appealing physique, the right amount of nutrients should be provided in what they eat. Be prepared to spend around $40 for a premium dog food which will last you about a month. Also, a monthly budget of at least $10 for treats should be set aside.

- **Grooming Supplies/Professional Service:** In order to

keep his skin and coat in good health, you can easily brush them up since they are known to be low – shedders but if you want to take them to a professional groomer you can set aside a budget of approximately $9 to $12.50 or more.

- **Routine Vet Checkup:** The cost for a vet visit is about $40. You can includes vaccinations, worm or tick preventions, and general routine checkup to prevent any potential disease that may harm your pet and cost more in the long run.

- **Pet Insurance/Emergency Care Fund:** you should set aside around $2,000 or more to cover any unexpected emergencies, vaccination, medications etc.

- **Other Accessories/Toys/Food Bowls:** Dog accessories are necessary if you want to take your dog out of the house. Accessories like a leash and other things like food/water materials, toys, and dog supplies. On average, extra accessories may cause at least $35 or more.

- **Travel Care:** You may need to shell out $100 or more for kennel care if you're travelling a lot.

Chapter Three: Acquiring Your Labradoodles

It's essential that before you purchase any dog for this matter, you should first consider on who takes care of them and how they are being taken care of, especially if they're still puppies. If you find a reputable breeder you can be sure to acquire a good dog breed.

This chapter will provide you with the criteria on selecting a healthy Labradoodle breed and how you can acquire it through a reputable dog breeder. You will also learn where to purchase these adorable puppies, and you can also check out the links provided if you wanted to purchase a dog online or if you need information on where to visit a particular dog breeder.

Recommended Reputable Breeders

Private Dog Breeders

Private dog breeders are people who breeds two dogs because they have purebred dogs or sometimes not purebred dogs, but they breed them for the sole purpose of selling them or they just want to have a litter.

The best thing about buying from these private dog breeders is quality assurance. You can pretty much gauge immediately if a breeder is good or not by simply going to their place and asking them questions. You can know how they raise animals and what kind of dog breeder they are plus you can also do some bargaining provided that you prove to them that you'll take care of their "babies"!

Rescue or Adoption

The major advantage is that these dogs may already be pre-prepped already by its previous owners. Sometimes they already received all the vaccines they need, may have been spayed/neuter already, may have undergone micro-chipping procedure, and sometimes already trained. However, you should still be careful when selecting from rescues especially in terms of the dog's health condition and/or behavior.

If you are the kind of person who loves to rescue animals from shelter and raise them properly that's a great thing to do, but you have to be quite an expert or you should have previous experience in purchasing from rescue centers especially when it comes to selecting a healthy breed which is why this may not work out for everyone. You should also be aware of additional adoption fees as well as proper documents before you can officially claim your chosen dog.

(Selected) Local Pet Shops

Buying from pet shops is not highly recommended because of the fact that some of them get their stock of puppies from a puppy mill. Take note that good breeders do not sell to pet stores.

Many dog organizations and breeders advise the public or potential dog keepers to stop purchasing from pet stores so that these pet stores will stop buying from puppy mills, and hopefully force them to completely stop breeding puppies and raise them in horrible conditions.

I'm not saying that all pet stores do the same thing but most of them are which is why it's important to keep that in mind if you're going to buy in the nearest pet shop. Never ever buy from a puppy mill because this is a place where puppies or dogs are kept in solely for breeding purposes. It does not provide an adequate living environment, and dogs are mostly under terrible conditions. Puppies bred from puppy mills have lots of illnesses because of the poor environment. These puppies are then purchased by pet stores and sold to people. What most people don't know is where exactly this dogs come from, and how are they raised since birth.

Characteristics of a Good Breeder

Good breeders show their dogs or joins dog competitions

It doesn't mean though that they need to join on a regular basis because there are a lot of hobby breeders out there that shows there dog occasionally because showing is quite expensive. Nevertheless, they should've at least showed their dogs once or twice. The main reason for this is because it evaluates a breeder's breeding stock, and it makes them conform to the breed standard.

If the breeder has a showing experience it's quite a proof that he/she is following the official breed standard, trains the dogs, maintain their health conditions, and also provide them with the care they need to have a sound temperament and good attitude towards people. If a breeder is showing their dogs, it also means that they are breeding a high - standard quality of dogs. Bad breeders, on the other hand, don't show their dogs because they pretty much don't care at all.

Good breeders are valuable source of information

You're not looking for a smart breeder or someone who has a degree relating to animal care, but as a reputable breeder, they should know everything there is to know about their particular breed. It's highly recommended that before you purchase anything, you should be able to interview them, and make a list of all the questions you think is relevant and will be helpful to you once you acquired a puppy.

Good breeders are more than welcome to answer all of your questions, and are also open to discussing things thoroughly. You can ask about the dog's pedigree, their history, their health, how much to feed a puppy, the do's and don'ts etc. Good breeders should also be there for the lifetime of your dogs, and they should be able to attend to any questions or concerns as well as show some interest on how their dog is doing after you have made the purchase. Make sure to establish a good relationship with your chosen breeder because he/she will be essential in raising healthy pups/dogs. Bad breeders may not be open to answer questions, and even if they do, they may not answer it in an expert manner.

Good breeders know when to let go of their new puppies

A good breeder knows the proper age of when they can let their puppies go to other homes. It's a major sign if you're dealing with a good breeder or a bad breeder. Any good breeder knows that puppies should be kept until 12 weeks old, bad breeders will sell puppies under 12 weeks old. Bad breeders are only after the money, they are not concern with their dogs.

Good breeders will provide good references

You can tell if the breeder is reputable if he/she gives good references from their past puppy owners or customers they'll be willing to give it to you as compared to bad breeders who will not because you may discover how irresponsible they are based from their previous clients.

Good breeders know everything about their dog's ancestry

When you ask them regarding the puppy's ancestry, a good breeder knows things in terms of the health conditions of the puppy's parents, their size issues, the puppy's grandparents, temperament etc. Bad breeders have no idea how the puppies came about, where they come from, their background, ancestral health issues and the likes. You'll have a better chance in acquiring a healthy dog because good breeders know the health history or genetic problems that may have been passed down from one generation to another as compared to backyard breeders.

Good breeders only breed to improve their dog breed

Good breeders usually just have a couple of litters a year. Bad breeders on the other hand will breed dogs just because they have them or they're going to have tons of litters because they wanted to make more money. Good breeders won't breed their dogs until they are sexually matured (around 2 years old) while bad breeders don't care about their age, and will breed their dogs as soon as they come in heat.

Good breeders sell their puppies with contracts

Good breeders will only sell to people with a limited spay/neuter contract. If you're interviewing a breeder and they tell you that they're going to sell a puppy without a contract, you are best moving on because that's a huge red flag. Good breeders want to make sure that they protect the breed, and they don't just let anybody breed their dogs because they care so much about their breed, they wanted to make sure that their dogs will go to responsible keepers.

A spay/neuter contract is done when selling a puppy to a new owner from a private/responsible/show breeder. When it comes to contracts, good breeders also offer a health guarantee. Another thing is that before sealing the deal with their pets, good breeders will also ask questions about you, and your family, and what you are looking for in a dog. You can also show them photos of your home, or your families, where you work etc. though not a lot of reputable breeders require that. The important thing is that they're really concern about where their breeds are going to go, and it's not about the money. You should also be sort of a "qualified keeper" and pass their personal standards so that they'll have a peace of mind that these pups will be well taken care of.

Good breeders offer a reasonable price for their puppies

Bad breeders usually sell very cheap puppies, and it's because they never made any sort of investment in it. You can easily tell if the breeder is irresponsible if he/she is selling a dog for a bargain or way below the average price for a certain breed. Whereas good breeders will sell their puppies at reasonable prices (not too cheap, and not too expensive). Good breeders are okay with selling their puppies at a high – end price because they know that their breeds are of quality, generally healthy, and are well – taken care of. They made investments to their pets like showing them to meet the official breed standard, and various medical testing to ensure that their puppies are strong and healthy. There's obviously more money involve both for the reputable breeder and the potential keeper, but you can be sure of a healthy breed, and save tons of cash and headaches in the long run.

Selecting a Healthy Breed

This section will give you information if your Labradoodle dog is healthy to keep because this breed is very prone to certain canine health problems and diseases. Keeping an eye for early signs of medical problems of your dog is of utmost importance; it could save you a lot of stress, time and money in the long run as well as your dog's longevity.

This basic checklist is what you need if you want to acquire a healthy pup. Doing so will ensure that you catch any sign of trouble as early as possible and prevent you from getting a sick animal.

- **Check the dog's bodies** - you should be doing a full body check of the pups/dogs. Just gently run your hand over all the parts the dog's body to see if there are any cuts, lumps, inflammation and any signs of discomfort.

Eyes: Eyes of dogs should be clear and the pupils should be of the same size. Check for ingrowing hair or eye lashes. Make sure also that there is no excessive discharge or signs of irritation among the pups.

Nose: The nose of dogs should be cool and moist. Keep an eye out for excessive sneezing, discharge and make sure that breathing is unobstructed and easy.

Mouth: You should also check the dog's mouth for anything out of the ordinary. The gums must be pink, if you see darker/redder patches, it may indicate a problem. You must also check for growths and lumps, and make sure that the teeth are clear. Observe also their breath as unusually bad breath could be an indication of digestive problems.

Ears: Check the ears of your dogs for wax build-up, bad odor, and swelling. This could be signs of ear infection or other health problems

Feet: Scrutinize a dog's feet for any grazes, cuts or growths.

- **Check their body movements** - watch the way the dogs moves and observe how they play, walk and run by themselves and with other dogs in the litter. Limping, excessive panting and mobility problems can be signs that the dog has internal problems.

- **Check their weight, height and general physical characteristics** – the dog should possess the right weight and height for its age. Being overweight or underweight is a huge problem among dogs. The breeder should make sure that he/she is feeding the pups a well-balanced diet to maintain a healthy physique, check if there's any sign of body defect as well.

Chapter Four: Habitat Requirements for Labradoodles

In this chapter you will learn the basics about your Labradoodle's habitat requirements including its shelter placement and housing needs. You will also learn some tips on how to dog - proof your house before your new pet arrives as well as some guidelines on how you can maintain an adequate living condition for them.

Providing your pet with a great environment is key in ensuring that your Labradoodle is happy and well – adjusted. Make them feel at home by also providing them lots of hugs and kisses! You can be rest assured that your pet will have a great time hanging out with you!

Ideal Habitat for Your Dog

Before anything else, when it comes to setting up the habitat for your Labradoodle, you need to consider the temperature. The ambient temperature in your house should be at a normal range, not too hot and not too cold either. You should also avoid exposing your dog to too much sunlight because it might cause skin or coat issues. Set the cage away from direct sunlight or cold temperatures, and it should also not be set up directly under air cons or heaters.

Next thing to consider is the position of the cage; your dog's cage should be ideally place in the familiar part of the house where there's "foot traffic" and not an isolated area. For designer dogs like the Labradoodle, you can set up a cage or a confinement area near the living room or probably near the couch where you hang out often.

When it comes to choosing the right cage size for your dog, the rule of thumb is to purchase a cage that is twice as large as the current size of your pet. After which, it is ideal to also buy a play pen and attached it to the crate so that your dog will have his/her own space and also an ample area for feeding, playing, and pooping. Whether your dog sleeps in your bed or their own bed is a matter for you to decide, as long as its sleeping place is cozy and sanitary.

The Bed, The Toys and the Dishes!

Labradoodles and most dogs in general only do three things in their whole life: eat, sleep and play! If your able to answer this basic needs then you can be considered a great keeper!

First of all, soft comfortable bedding should be placed inside your dog's crate especially if you're going to leave your Labradoodle for a long period.

The crate should be the place where your dog will feel comfortable sleeping in because it will help teach your puppy to be comfortable in his confinement area. It's also ideal that you provide a blanket so your dog can cuddle up with it or to provide added comfort. You might also want to provide your pet with its own snuggle puppy – these are plush toys with a realistic heartbeat and warming pet that simulates another puppy and helps in comforting younger puppies to transition from their breeder to being part of a family or as a household pet.

You can also provide other dog toys (at least 4 to 6) to stimulate your Labradoodle. Alternate the toys every week or every now and then, or find out what toy your pet prefers. It's also best to supply a variety of toys serve for different purposes to keep your puppy interested. Always supervise your pets while he/she is playing its toys.

Aside from a plush toy you can purchase some kind of chewing toys to satisfy your dog's instinct to chew, and also relieve pressurized gums. There are also toys that you can buy to stimulate your dog's senses; these toys have varying colors, sounds, or smells. Rubber squeaky and puzzle toys can also be ideal because they are fun, noisy and also provide mental and physical stimulation especially for young pups. Your pup may cry for some nights – a ticking clock or a radio playing softly can be a comfort.

You need to provide your dog with ample drinking water, and food bowls especially if you're going away for a certain period of time. Most owners recommend a non – breakable, non – spill water bowl otherwise your puppy or dog will spill its water, and will be left with no water for days while you are away. You can also buy a ceramic or glass water/food bowls, however it is only ideal if you are at home because if in case the puppy breaks it, he/she might ingest the broken pieces or injure its food with the shattered glass. A stainless food and water dishes are also ideal because it's durable and also quite easy to clean. It's also safe for your pet, but it can be tipped over as well.

Setting Up a Toilet Area

The pooping area inside the play pen should be located on the opposite side of your dog's sleeping area. You should make sure that the space is far away as possible from their crate or from where you are feeding them.

If you have done some potty training already outside on the grass, and you want to train your pet to pee or poo inside its own play pen, you might want to consider buying a synthetic grass from your local hardware store. You might want to put the synthetic grass in a tray or buy a synthetic interlocking grass tiles.

The synthetic interlocking grass tile is very ideal because it has drainage holes to prevent fluids from flowing; you just have to replace a puppy pee pad underneath it to soak up the excess fluids. Whenever you're cleaning the synthetic grass, you can just hose it down, and let it dry for a while. You can buy more than two square grasses so that you have a spare while you are drying the other set after cleaning it.

The toileting sofa should be removed if you are at home, and should only be provided when you're away. The reason for this is that you want to avoid tolerating the puppy that it's okay to toilet indoors; ensure that your pet poo or pee outdoors at every possible opportunity to accelerate toilet training.

A plastic airline create with a wire front door is an excellent aid in toilet training your dog and also provides a secure den for them to sleep in. Puppies resist soiling their beds, so it will rapidly learn to hold on overnight and the cage will allow you to take your puppy to where you want it to poo every morning - with the reasonable expectation that it will indeed go. Take your pup out before you go to bed, them put them to bed. Then take the puppy out to its toilet area first thing in the morning.

Tips on How to Dog – Proof Your House

Dog proofing is similar to baby proofing; this should be done before your pet arrives or before you take them home. Protect your Labradoodle pup from various household hazards to eliminate any unwanted accidents or situations. Here are some tips on how to dog – proof your house:

- Provide fences, a screened porch or a safe enclosure. Be sure to dog-proof your yard so that your dog could experience the outdoors safely.

- Remove any poisonous plants since dogs are

naturally curious, and likes to chew anything. If your dog chew any plants, even the non-poisonous ones can cause vomiting and diarrhea or fatality.

- Install padded perches indoors near a window frame or in your patio so that your pet could enjoy and hang out but do not leave your doors and screens unlocked.

- Do not leave your appliances plugged, as mentioned earlier, they will chew anything including electric wires, not only is this potentially fatal for your dog but also a dangerous threat for your home.

- Buy a harness and train your dog to walk on a leash when going around the neighborhood.

- Consider buying a ready-made dog tree to provide climbing opportunities for your dog inside.

- Make sure to keep lots of dog toys out and put anything precious and destructible away.

- Make sure to keep away toxic liquids or materials like cleaning supplies or other household items that can harm them.

- Make sure that your puppy will not be able to enter bathrooms or kitchens alone because it can be dangerous for them.

- Once your dog arrives, you can observe it as it explores and become familiar with your home, you'll and also get to discover some things you need to dog – proof.

Chapter Five: Food for Your Labradoodle

Feeding your Labradoodle is not that complicated but you have to make sure that its level of activity, age, and weight should be taken into consideration to meet its nutritional diet needs. Labradoodles should be given the right amount of recommended food for a balanced nutrition because proper diet can lengthen the life expectancy of your dog, protect them from serious illnesses and also keep up their energy levels. In this chapter, you'll learn the majority of your pet's nutritional needs as well as some feeding guidelines, and foods that are good and harmful for your dog. They will become what you feed them.

Nutritional Needs of Labradoodles

Most dogs are always hungry because as dogs evolved they have adapted to the 'feast and famine' principle which means that they are genetically programmed to eat everything in sight because the pack might not make another kill for weeks. Good quality commercial pet food offers a perfectly balanced diet in every meal. You can choose to place a small amount of food available as a snack, whenever your dog feels like nibbling.

If you decide to use commercial food for your puppy, you should feed him/her top quality dry puppy food until 4 months. Do not change your pup's diet for at least 4 - 5 days. The puppy may not eat that much especially if he/she just got to its new home. You have to keep in mind that your puppy has been through considerable stress and change in the last few days which also means that he could be predispose to diarrhea - a sudden change of diet at this stage will almost certainly result in gastric upset.

Most canned food has relatively more fat, protein and animal products and lesser carbohydrates than dry and semi-moist food. Pet food labels must list the percentage of protein, fat, fibre, and water in the food. Ask your veterinarian on how to properly read pet food labels so that you can get the most out of the food.

Feeding your dog dry food has two major benefits; the first one is that since it is dry, it won't eat a lot of food which of course would prevent overeating that could lead to obesity; and the second is that it will keep its teeth stronger because of chewing. Be reminded that dry foods should not be the only type of food for your dog's entire diet; you should also feed them fresh ingredients.

Animal Bones for Your Labradoodle

Whether feeding homemade or commercial food I recommend a raw bone each day. Bones should be raw, lean and from young animals - lamb or chicken lamb rib bones and chicken carcasses are great because your dog will eat all of it and will not make your place look like a graveyard.

Raw bones are a good source of calcium and vitamins and it also keeps a dog's teeth and in good condition; a big bone will give your dog hours of pleasure as well. Your puppy will love chicken bones and if the pieces are small, they will swallow it whole, so it is better to give larger pieces that do not need to be chewed up.

Remember that dog nutrition is not difficult to figure out, and that every meal every day does not need to be perfectly balance but a raw bone each day is an essential part of a healthy balanced homemade diet.

Feeding and Brand Selection

- Don't use food to show your affection. Tidbits should only be used as rewards for good behavior in training; the best treat you can give your dog is your company.

- Cooked bones are poorly digested, may splinter and shouldn't be fed.

- If you feed bones or table scraps, reduce the amount of dry food you give your dog.

- Buy dog foods at small independent pet supply stores because supermarkets, groceries, superstores and the likes sometimes don't carry quality dog foods.

- Look at the product label of the brand you chose, and examine its ingredients list. What you need to look out for are top – quality, and whole ingredients.

- It's not recommended that you buy foods containing proteins or fats from unknown or unnamed species. You should buy whole ingredients that come from named or known species such as duck, lamb, beef, chicken, and the likes.

- Organ meats are by – products, so if a food contains organs of top – quality, it should be added in the ingredients list and named separately. An example is beef heart and lamb liver, otherwise avoid buying that particular dog food.

- You should also look for whole grains, and carbohydrate sources like barley, quinoa, sweet potatoes, and wheat. As much as possible avoid processed carbs like brewers rice or wheat mill.

- Pet food formulators sometimes use one or two food fractions for specific purpose like dried beet pulp or tomato pulp as a fiber source to improve the quality of the dog's stool however, if the entire ingredients list of that particular brand is comprised of nothing but food formulators, then you should stop purchasing it or avoid it in the first place because it might be inexpensive but it is an over-processed food, and it's not good for your dog's health.

- Don't buy foods that contain artificial colors or sweeteners because dogs, like humans, have sweet receptors but it's not beneficial to your pets overall health. The purpose of sweeteners is to increase the palate ability of the food, but if the food already has the quality, your dog won't need the sugar. It can also contribute to diabetes in the long run.

- Don't buy foods that are preserved with artificial preservatives. However, natural preservatives don't preserve foods for as long as the artificial ones.

- Make sure to check the dates on the bag. You should know the date of manufacture and the expiration date of the dog food. Each manufacturer sets the date by which the food will still be somehow fresh, wholesome, and full of vitamins and minerals that can degrade overtime.

- Don't purchase any product that is naturally preserved and marked with the code or date that suggest the food is good for more than a year. You should opt to buy a dog food that is recently manufactured.

- You should also look for a product that best matched your dog's need for protein, fat, and calories. Since Labradoodles are active and small pets, you may want to buy a high fat, and high protein dog food.

- Make sure to go to your vet and follow their advice regarding the contents of the dog food that is best for your pet's condition.

- Obesity is the most common health problem facing pet dogs today so to avoid over feeding, just remember that being lean is healthy.

Recommended Food Brands for Labradoodles

Feeding your dog a specific diet can make your pet's physique stay stronger, and strengthen its immune system to protect him/her against illnesses especially as they get older. Below are 3 of the most recommended dog food brands for your Labradoodles.

Canidae Grain Free Pure Dog Food

Canidae Grain Free Pure is mostly a plant – based meal, a favorite brand among Labradoodles and based from many dog keepers they are indeed a quality dog food product. This dry food contains about 33% protein, 13% fat and 45% carbs. The ratio of the fat and the protein is around 49% which means that the brand contains near average carbohydrates, fat and protein compared to most dry dog kibbles. Considering the protein effects of veggies like flaxseed and peas, this dry kibble pretty much contains a moderate amount of meat, not to mention that the animal meats used as ingredients are 'named meats' which is why this food brand is highly recommended for Labradoodles.

Main Ingredients:

Turkey Meal: It is a concentration of turkey meat that has around 300% more protein source than a cooked turkey.

Sweet Potato: A major source of carbs in dog foods, the sweet potato ingredient is Gluten – free, rich in beta carotene and also fiber that helps in digestion.

Peas: Another good source of carbs and fiber, peas are another major ingredient which makes this brand suited for Labradoodles.

Potato: Gluten – free source and also contains a significant amount of calories for dogs.

Tomato Pomace: It's actually a 'leftover' of a tomato after being process for other food source like catsup, juice or soup. Nevertheless, it's very high in fiber, has nutritious content and it's also a cheaper food filler.

Flaxseed: Contains omega – 3 fatty acids and it's also rich is soluble fiber.

Salmon Oil: Another type of omega – 3 fatty acids that also contain EPA and DHA which are the most needed type of fats both for dogs and humans.

Chicory Root – an ingredient that makes the Canidae Grain Free Pure brand unique contains high levels of inulin that has lots of carbs, high in fiber and also prebiotic to enable a healthy growth of good bacteria that could aid in the dog's digestion.

Acana Regionals Dog Food

The Acana Regionals Brand is another great quality meat – based dog food for your Labradoodle. It contains 34% of protein, 39% carbs and 19% fats. The ratio of the fat and the protein is around 54%. It has many source of protein from named meats as well as nutritious meat meals combination, another highly recommended dog food brand.

Main Ingredients:

Chicken Meal: It's the major ingredient of the brand and much more nutritious than a fresh chicken since it's a concentration of chicken meat.

Barley: This ingredient provides high levels of fiber and carbohydrates.

Oatmeal: Naturally rich in fiber and B – vitamins, oatmeal is another great ingredient made from ground oats that are also gluten – free.

Whole dried egg: Eggs is a great source of nutrients for dogs, and they are also easy to digest. It comes in a dehydrated powder mixed with other ingredients in this food brand.

Chicken: Even if it's a good source of nutrients, the chicken contained in the package will lose almost all its moisture once cooked and may only account for a smaller portion of the total ingredients.

Chicken Fat: This ingredient is high in omega – 6 fatty acid and also contains high levels of linoleic acid. It's a quality ingredient that your dog needs and it is obtained by getting the juice of the chicken.

Potato: this ingredient helps in digestion, contains a fair amount of carbs and also gluten – free.

Brown Rice: another source of carbohydrates for dogs although it may not have that much significance to the brand's overall nutritional value.

Alfalfa meal – Contain fiber and high levels of protein

American Natural Premium Dog Food

American Natural Premium Dog Food has 28% protein, 19% fat and 45% carbs. It's mean fat level is around 17%. And the ratio of fat and protein is about 61%. It's another plant – based dog food that mostly contains chicken and lamb meals as well as fish meals.

Menhaden Fish Meal: menhaden fishes are small fishes found in the ocean, they have high levels of omega – 3 fatty acids and protein. These kinds of fish are deep water species which is an advantage because that means that they are not at risk of being contaminated with mercury. They are usually found in the tissues of whole fish that are not decomposed or fish cuttings used in factories/production.

Legumes and Lentils: both of these ingredients are a source of fiber and carbohydrates but you should also consider that they contain about 25% protein which is a factor that also needs to be considered.

Dried fermentation products: it provides enzymes which are good for digestion

Chelated Minerals: These minerals are chemically attached to protein foods that also help in absorption. It's usually found in quality dog foods.

How to Properly Feed Your Dog

- Follow the Feeding Instructions and Recommended Daily Feeding Amounts on the packaging of your pet food. You can also consult your veterinarian regarding the feeding measurement.

- Place the recommended food inside the bowl or dish every day so that your Labradoodle can eat anytime he/she pleases.

- Use a shallow bowl that your dog can grab food from easily. Try placing the dish in the open to maximize sight lines. It also helps lessen the tension.

- You can find also buy food accessories at your local pet store or even online. Its costs vary depending on the brand of the product

- Always check the feeders after use to make sure your dog is actually eating the recommended daily amount of food.

- For high – energy dogs like the Labradoodle just divide the bowls into several portions so he can nibble them in any part of the house.

- Make sure that your Labradoodle is properly hydrated.

- You should feed your pup three times a day until it is 3 – 3 ½ months old, twice daily until 5 – 6 months old and then once daily after that.

Chapter Six: Grooming Your Labradoodle

In terms of grooming, you may want to take this seriously because even if the coats of Labradoodles are hypoallergenic, they are long - coated dogs. Other basic grooming needs like clipping their toes, brushing their teeth, and cleaning their ears are also necessary part of your dog's hygiene. In this chapter you'll learn some tips on how to groom them and maintain their fluffy appearance while making sure that they are neat and tidy.

How to Cut Your Labradoodle's Hair

When you start the grooming technique, make sure to use a Number 10 blade as well as an E – comb.

Body

- Start shaving the hair at the base of your Labradoodle's skull and work your way down from there – through its body, legs and down on its back as well as the sides and its tummy.

- Once you get to the rump or your dog's back portion, you should make sure that you pull back its tail inwards or between its legs before combing the back side to make sure you're smoothing out any curly hairs

Eyes

- Use a thinning shear or a straight scissors to avoid blood clots in the eye

- Just carefully cut the corner of the eyes (about ½ inch down) both on the right and left side so that it is clean and well – blended

Ears

- Comb the hair in the ears downward
- **Back Portion:** Using your straight scissors carefully cut the hair on the ears starting on its back portion until the tip of your Labradoodle's ear.
- **Front Portion:** Cut the hair halfway down the ear and make sure that you don't cut it too far the ear and remove too much hair
- **Ear Tip:** Cut the hairs found on the tip of the ear and just curve it or shaped it

Head

- **Top:** Comb your dog's hair back resembling a ponytail; put your fingers in an angle just about 1 inch off the base of your dog's skull.
- **Front/Bangs:** Comb your entire dog's hair forward, and using your thinning shears, just cut an inverted V – shape above your dog's nose or between its eyes to expose the clean look of your dog's eye.

Cutting Hairs in Your Dog's Sanitary Portion

- You will use again the Number 10 blade, make your dog stand up and hold its front legs so you can easily access their bellies and private areas and do a haircut underneath.

- Make sure to carefully clip underneath its belly and in between the legs in its private parts.
- When clipping its bum area, be careful not to clip too short and not too far off the tail to not expose their rectum portion too much.

Paws and Foot

- Before cutting it up, you should first comb all the hair on its foot and around the paw pads downwards
- Turn your Labradoodle's foot over to be able to cut that area using the Number 10 blade
- Be careful in cutting the hair on its paws as to not expose too much of the foot underneath
- After doing that in all of its paws, make sure to brush the hair down again to straighten it out and also clip using scissors all the remaining hair around its paws to make sure that it is nice and clean.

Muzzle

- Comb all the hair forward, and using your shears just cut the hair that are longer and seems irregular in its muzzle to its beard. This could shape your dog's nose and clean it up.

- Make sure to also clip the excess hairs or uneven hairs to tidy up your entire grooming process.

Cutting the Toenails

Make sure to clip your Labradoodle's toenails with dog toenail clippers once every six or eight weeks. It will keep your dog's paws clean and healthy and will prevent him from scratching upon jumping up. Be sure not to cut their nails too close as this may hurt them.

Brushing the Teeth

You have to thoroughly brush your Labradoodles' teeth on a regular basis as this type of breed is prone to dental cavities. You have to use special toothpaste that contains enzymes to inhibit bacterial growth in the mouth.

Chapter Seven: Training Your Labradoodle

Labradoodles are very energetic pets. They're like "dogs in steroids," which is why if you don't instill discipline and train them while they're still puppies, they could be really tough to handle when they grow up. This chapter can make you understand the science behind a dog's behavior and how their natural instincts in the wild can be beneficial in making them well – mannered dogs but not at the expense their playful personalities. You'll also get to learn some socialization strategies to implement at every life stage to make sure that your pet is well – trained.

Dog Behavior

Dogs are pack animals, which is why they adapt so well to human society- they are adapted to cope with a complex set of relationships. The relationship between dogs and humans is remarkable and has been going on for so long that some scientists suggest dogs have affected human evolution just as we have quite clearly affected theirs. In the wild, dogs live in social groups which are hierarchical, with a dominant dog (usually a male) and its subordinates. These hierarchies are designed to prevent social discord by ensuring that everyone knows their place. In your home, it will come to see your family as its pack. Your pup must learn its place in the pecking order of your pack and that place must be at the bottom, the good news is that there are many painless ways of asserting your dominance over your dog.

A dog's behavior is a combination of instant and acquired or learned behavior and dogs go through developmental stages just as people do. Dogs must learn by trial and error, they try something – if the outcome is rewarding they are more likely to do it again – if the outcome is unpleasant they are less likely to do it again. The more often they have a pleasant outcome from a behavior the more rapidly they will learn to perform that behavior.

Socialization Period

For Puppies: 7 Weeks to 4 Months of Age

During this period your pup progresses from an equivalent of a human toddler – about 4 years of age, needing security and reassurance and could also be prone to tantrums. Like most toddlers they need naps – in fact they sleep most of the time for the first few weeks and dogs in general spend a lot more time sleeping than humans. No wonder why puppies like Labradoodles always have that very high energy all the time.

Socialization is very important in any dog's life. It is the time where a puppy learns what it means to be a dog, who its family is and where it fits in the family hierarchy. It is a time when one bad experience can permanently affect its personality; phobias to things like travel and vacuum cleaners can develop at this stage.

During this period your pup should be exposed to as many different non-threatening experiences as possible. You should avoid any punishment that might frighten your puppy. Remember that no matter how irritating it may be, it is only a baby which is why punishment is usually an ineffective training tool.

If you have young children, you can let them carry the puppy around as much as they like. If you think about it toddlers are too close to the ground to do too much damage if they drop them, and even small children can learn to carry a puppy safely. The pups begin to learn from this that the child, who may soon be not much bigger than it is, is the boss. This is the most important lesson a pup must learn, and this learning starts in the socialization period. A family dog must be at the bottom of the family pack.

For Juveniles (3 - 18 Months)

The best thing that can be said about juvenile dogs in general is that they grow out of it! This is the time when your dog discovers the joy of digging and chewing. It's the time when it's fatal to leave shoes at the door, clothes on the floor and hoses lying on the lawn. It is also a good time to put your gardening plans on hold! They will destroy them! They're like crazy teenagers at this point, they're at the peak of their lives, they can do anything they want – and get away with it! And because they're Labradoodles, they're 10 times more energetic than the average juvenile dog.

Unfortunately, this is also the age when many people change their minds about owning a dog and when a lot of this young pups end up being put down in pounds and animal shelters because they're too much to handle. Patience, training and more patience are needed to get through this period. Remember that when your pup is on its own it will be excited to see you, and so the more time it spends alone, the more excited it will be. If you find your Labradoodle too active when it is outside alone – it will continue to be just as excited inside the house. This is why you must train your Labradoodle pup to behave calmly inside, and only allow rough play and excitement outside.

Adulthood (18 Months – 2 Years Onwards)

Asserting your dominance should really be regarded as teaching your dog good manners because manners just like the hierarchical behavior of the dog pack mentioned earlier are the 'social lubricant' that holds everything in social situations.

In a dog pack the dominant dog will set the rules, in the family pack a dog with good manners is a dog that accepts that you and your family have rules and that these rules are decided on by you! A dog which does this is safe to be trusted with your family. A polite person will wait for others to enter before barging through the front door and a polite dog which knows and understands the family hierarchy must be taught to do the same. Just as you teach your children to wait until everyone is seated, you should teach your dog patience at the food bowl.

A dominant or undisciplined dog always grabs the food before anyone else, and may not be patient – this could eventually result to aggressiveness especially whenever they're hungry and you make them wait. Feed your dog only after the family has eaten, and never feed a dog from your plate.

Once the pup is sitting politely feed him/her from your hand. A low growl accompanied by a severe cute puppy stare can be very effective but if you need to discipline your pup and make them remember it, you should 'NO,' firmly or simply ignore this "cute puppy tantrums." Puppies are like toddlers with their endless cry of "look at me," so withdrawal of any contact like folding up your arms, standing up or looking away as if the puppy isn't there at all could be a very effective tool for controlling your dogs and instilling discipline. The key in handling your dog's behavior is to discipline them while they're still young.

House and Potty Training

Dog behavior is formed by trial and error. The exception to this is toilet training, which is largely shaped by habit. Pups become house trained by developing a habit. It usually takes about 2-4 weeks of constant vigilance. You need to know a few facts about elimination behavior. Pups are most likely to defecate and urinate after sleep, after a meal or after exercise. When they are about to poo, they will sniff the ground and may walk in circles; there may also be a little warning before they urinate.

They will try very hard not to wee and poo in their own beds unless they are confined too long. Once they have started using one place they are likely to keep using it because of the smell, your Labradoodle will have preferred toilet places which are why they will often seek out a carpet.

As soon as you get home on your first day, take your pup to the designated place in your garden and wait there patiently until they relieve themselves. From then on take your pup outside, to the place you have chosen, as soon as it wakes up in the morning, after a sleep, after a meal, and whenever it begins to walk around sniffing the ground and at least every 2 hours throughout the day.

If it urinates or poops in the designated toilet area, make sure to praise him/her or give it a food reward this way it could have a positive reinforcement. If you catch your pup in the act inside the house say "No" firmly, pick it up and take it to the place you have chosen for it to use. If you are too late clean up the mess, use soap and water and then an enzymatic cleanser to get rid of the smell so that your Labradoodle will not relieve themselves in that area again.

As mentioned earlier, a freight cage – a plastic shell with a wire front door – is a great tool that most newbie keepers use to do toilet training. Your pup will hold on as long as possible rather than poo in its bed and a couple of nights should be enough to train it to sleep through. Take it out last thing at night and first thing in the morning and you will have control over its elimination behavior at least once each morning.

If your Labradoodle make a mess inside the house or its cage, don't punish your puppy because it could affect its behavior even more. Puppies cannot make the connection that there's a poop on the rug and your angry about it. Never rub its nose in it – the pup will have no idea whatsoever why you are doing this and will not learn from the experience. If you are careful and really take the time to discipline your dog, he/she should be house trained in about two weeks or in just a month.

Training Tips for Your Labradoodles

This section will give you some tips on how to train your dog to behave properly inside and outside the house. Here are some guidelines to keep in mind:

- Respect training is the first thing you should teach your dog before you potty train them or teach them how to do some cool tricks. As previously mentioned, you need to be able to establish an authoritative attitude when training Labradoodles otherwise you'll have a hard time controlling them.

- Leash training can also be ideal as this will eventually allow him to go wherever he wants.

- It's also advisable that you enroll your pet in some kind of handling classes; professional trainers will teach your dog to walk or stand beside you, and teach them how to behave properly.

- If you want to show your dog or join dog competitions; conformation classes is also recommended. This is for the purpose of making your dog mimic you which can be effective if you sign them up in competitions. These classes will surely help you learn and fine tune all the skills that are required in a show ring.

- When it comes to litter training, what you can do every time your dog pees or poops, is to call out his/her name to cause him to pause, and focus your attention to you.

- As your Labradoodle is relieving itself, repeat a chosen word or phrase so that he can associate it with his actions. Some owners use poopy, potty or toilet etc.

- Bring your dog outside with a specific schedule. If you are heading outside to get some exercise, bring him to his bathroom area first. It is highly recommended to have a harness. If you are not used to having one, you may at first think that they are difficult to take on and off, as you go along of course, it will become easier.

- Allow your pup at least five minutes to find the perfect spot within the area, and for his bladder and bowel muscles to relax.

- If your pup is done peeing in the right spot, offer the reward treat right away. Always give praise to them at the same time.

If your pup misses the 'bathroom area,' don't punish him or her right away. They'll eventually learn in their own time. Make sure to clean the area with an enzyme cleanser.

Chapter Eight: Breeding Your Labradoodles

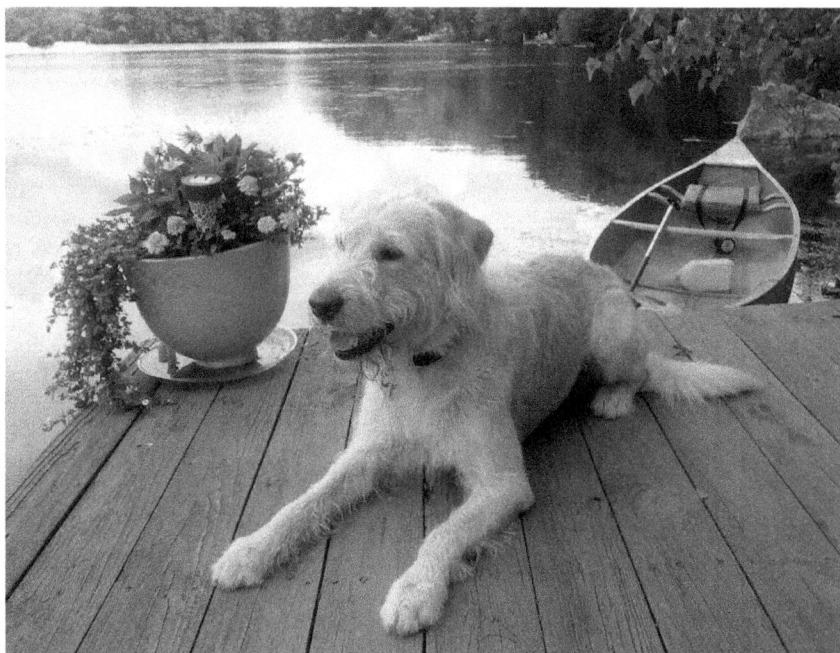

Breeding Labradoodles can sound fun and interesting but before you try your hands on it, I want to personally advise you to not do it by yourself especially if you're just a newbie. It's probably best to leave it by a professional or better yet learn from someone who has experience. The breeding process is not simple and you could risk the health factor of your Labradoodle if you don't do it properly. Nevertheless, it's still something you need to have knowledge on so that when you let other people do it, you'll have an idea if they're doing the right thing.

In this chapter you'll be provided with information about the breeding basics of Labradoodles, their pre and post mating process, labor period, and some guidelines on how to raise puppies after birth and during the weaning time.

Important Reminders About Breeding

It is important that you wait until the female reaches sexual maturity before you start breeding them. Most breeders recommend waiting until two years old to start breeding, though some dogs reach their full size even before they turn two years of age. This is an assurance that the dog is mature enough to physically carry and bear puppies, but it also provides enough time for any serious health problems to be spotted.

Before six months of age, several dog organizations recommend having your dogs neutered or spayed. This is the time where the female dog experiences her first heat. The cycle is usually twenty days. What may be normal for one dog may differ from another.

If you want to increase your chances of a successful breeding, you need to keep track of your Labradoodle's estrus cycle. Once your female reaches the point of ovulation, you can introduce her to the male dog and let nature take its course. Breeding behavior varies slightly from one breed to another, but you can expect the male dog to mount the female from behind after her heat cycle. If the breeding is successful, conception will occur and the gestation period will begin.

Once you see your dog having signs of congenital heart problems, it is more preferable to not breed her for a year or so. Dogs should only be bred preferably every other year. Consecutive conception and giving birth within a short span of time causes problems in her reproductive system and could result to a high level of loss in puppies. This is caused by different kinds of reasons, and can also happen in any breed not only among Labradoodles, but this happens more often in designer breeds.

Pre – Mating Period

First Few Days: During the first day of heating, you might notice some changes like the swelling of your dog's vulva because of the reddish discharge coming out; you'll also notice that she is constantly licking its rear.

Next 5 Days: The main physical change you'll notice is the continuous swelling of its vulva and a blood discharge like a menstruation in female humans.

In 10 Days: The color of your dog's vulva lightens up a bit, and the vulva will have a moist or soft appearance.

In 14 Days: Your dog's vulva will become clear, and its edges will begin to harden up. Swelling and discharge will be almost gone as well. This will continue until the 21st day, by then it means that your female dog or bitch is ready for mating.

21 Days Onwards: When a female dog or what they termed it as the bitch is in heat, there are a few signs that can point towards her beginning this process such as being nervous, easily distracted, some signs of increasing appetite, and urinating more than usual. Male dogs in general are ready to breed from the age of eighteen months to five years old. Your female dog's personality may also alter due to the abrupt change in her hormones.

Post – Mating Period

Gestation Period (first few 2 weeks after mating): After the male dog fertilizes the egg inside the female's body, the gestation period will start in the female dogs. During that cycle, the puppies start to develop inside her womb of the female dog. The gestation period of Labradoodles averages 63 days. The gestation period is the period of time following conception during which the puppies develop in the mother's uterus.

In 3 weeks: You won't be able to tell if your dog is pregnant until after the third week. By the twenty-fifth day of the pregnancy it is safe for the vet to perform an ultrasound. By this time, you need to take special care of your dog's nutrient to make sure that she is properly nourished. It is generally best to offer your dog free feeding because she will know how much she needs to eat. Make sure your dog's diet is high in protein as well as calories, calcium, and fat to support the development of her puppies.

In 4 weeks: On the twenty - eight day, the vet should be able to feel the puppies by palpating the female's abdomen.

In 5 weeks: By this time, you already need to make changes to your dog's diet, make sure that you slightly increase her daily rations in an amount proportionate to her weight gain.

In 6 weeks: An X-ray can be performed to check the size of the litter. The average litter size of Labradoodle is 8, with a range of 4 to 10 puppies. Keep in mind that new mothers will often have smaller litters but you can expect that the next few litters will generally be larger before the litter size starts to taper off again. By this time, you should have also set up a whelping box where your female dog can comfortably give birth to her puppies. Place the box in a quiet, dim area and line it with newspapers and old towels for comfort. The closer it gets to giving birth, the more time your dog will spend in the whelping box because she is also preparing it for her litter.

Labor Period

After about 63 days: By this time your Labradoodles starts going into labor, you'll easily notice it because you'll see obvious signs of discomfort. Your dog might start pacing restlessly, panting, and switching positions.

Prior to Labor Time: Your dog's body temperature may drop as low as 98°F (36.6°C); the normal dog temperature is 100°F to 102°F (37.7°C to 38.8°C). Contractions will occur as often as 10 minutes apart. If your pet has contractions for more than 2 hours without any of the puppies being born, contact your veterinarian immediately.

During Labor: Once your dog starts giving birth, the puppies will arrive about every thirty minutes following ten to thirty minutes of straining.

After Birth

First Few Hours: After giving birth the mother dog will lick its puppy clean; it may even eat the umbilical cord since it is animal instinct. This also helps to stimulate the puppy to start breathing on his own. Once all of the puppies have been born, the mother will expel the rest of the placenta then let the puppies start nursing.

Nursing Period: It is essential that the puppies begin nursing within one hour of being born because this is when they will receive the colostrum from the mother. Colostrum is the first milk produced from the puppy's mother. It contains a variety of nutrients as well as antibodies to protect the pups until their own immune systems develop.

Weaning Period

First few weeks of puppies: In the first few weeks of the puppy's life, they will be highly dependent on their mother until they start to become fully mobile. New born Labradoodles weighs small but of course they will continue growing and maturing until they reach their adult size. To keep tract of the growth of your puppies, it is ideal to weigh them weekly. You also need to place the puppies on a warm place because the hair that they have is not enough to make them warm.

After 12 Days: The eyes and ears of the newborn Labradoodles will start to open. As the puppies grow, they will start to become increasingly active and they will grow very quickly as long as they are properly fed by their mother or by you.

Next 6 weeks (after birth): Once they hit 6 weeks old you can start weaning them. Start offering your puppies a small amount of solid food that is soaked in broth or water. The puppies might sample small bits of solid food even while they are still nursing

In about 8 to 10 weeks (after birth): After a few weeks, the puppies will be completely weaned which means that your Labradoodle is ready to be separated from their mother. If you plan to sell the puppies, be sure not to send them home unless they are fully weaned at least 8 weeks old.

10 weeks and older: By this time, you as a keeper should start taking steps in socializing the puppies from an early age to make sure they turn into well - adjusted adults.

Chapter Nine: Common Diseases and Health Requirements

It is not enough that you know the basic information of a Labradoodle, you must also be aware of potential threats and disease that could harm your pet. Of course, you want your dog to live the longest life possible and with that said, health care should never be neglected and taken for granted. In this chapter you will be provided with some of the most common health problems affecting Labradoodle. You as the potential dog keeper should also learn how to strengthen your dog's resistance to common illnesses by giving them the necessary vaccinations and through having regular checkup with their vets.

Common Health Problems

In this section, you will learn about the diseases that may affect and threaten your Labradoodles. Learning these diseases as well as its remedies is vital for you and your dog so that you could prevent it from happening or even help with its treatment in case they caught one.

Common Diseases for Puppies

Roundworm, Tapeworm and Heartworm

Pups should be treated every two weeks from birth until they are 12 weeks of age for roundworm and from 8 weeks of age for tapeworm. After 12 weeks of age they should be treated for tapeworm and roundworm every month until they are 6 months old. As adults they should be treated routinely every 3 months. Heartworm is a mosquito borne blood parasite of dogs, which are the cause of severe illness and death.

To prevent parasite infection, it requires a tablet either daily or monthly, a spot on product, or an annual injection on adult dogs. This parasite is now prevalent throughout the world. You should be aware of the disease and should use a preventative drug regularly and discuss it with your veterinarian during the puppy's 12 week veterinary visit.

Fleas

Fleas are a common summer problem. There is evidence that dogs which are kept flea free for the first 12 months of their lives are unlikely to develop flea allergy. Your pup has not been exposed to fleas. Bath your pet every 14 or 30 days using soap free shampoo and apply a top spot residual flea control every 30 days. Use Frontline, Advantix, Revolution or other brands your vet will suggest. Do not use tea tree oil, human soaps or shampoos.

Ticks

The coastal paralysis tick can kill puppies! It is essential that you use preventative measures as also check your dog daily if you live in a tick area. Make sure to discuss tick control with your local veterinarian in order to determine the seriousness of the risk in your area so that you will be aware of the appropriate preventative measures.

Common Diseases for Adult Labradoodles

Minor Problems

Vomiting

Many things can cause vomiting in dogs; it can either be a viral infection or bacteria as well as parasites and even inflammation of pancreas. Younger dogs could sometimes swallow foreign objects they should not ingest; these things can get stuck in the stomach or digestive tract that could cause inflammation. Your dog may also vomit if he/she eats foods like grapes that can cause renal disease. If your puppy is vomiting make sure to go to the vet as soon as possible because compared to adult dogs, puppies are much weaker, and this means that they can get dehydrated even faster. Vomiting can cause damage to the esophagus of both young and adult dogs so better get a cure from it to prevent further consequences.

Ear Infection

Most dogs including Labradoodles will have an ear infection during their lifetime. Ear infection is often caused by moisture of the ear which can be breeding grounds for bacteria or yeast. Sometimes it can also be caused by bathing, grooming or whenever your dog is swimming. Summer is usually the time when this disease is prevalent, that's when you notice redness in your dog's ear or a very strong odor. Fortunately, it's also something that is treatable, you can just buy a drop or sometimes the vet will require antibiotics. Even if this is not a serious problem, you should still take your dog to the vet for medical attention because you want to keep this infection just outside the ear and prevent it from further spreading into its ear canal because it can be harder to treat.

Arthritis

Arthritis is very common among designer breeds. Your Labradoodle can develop arthritis as they grow older or as they age. It actually increases its effect, if a dog is born with hip dysplasia. The good news is that, it is a manageable condition, and it's best to get an early diagnosis from your vet. If you want to prevent your Labradoodle in suffering from arthritis, the best you can do is to maintain its diet, and keep him/her as lean as possible. Medications can aid your dog if ever he/she develops arthritis but doctors suggest that good exercise and proper diet is essential.

Major Problems:

<u>Hip Dysplasia</u>

Hip dysplasia is a very common musculoskeletal problem among small breed of dogs like the Labradoodle. In a normal hip, the part of the thigh bone sits snugly within the groove of the hip joint and it rotates freely within the grove as the dog moves. Hip dysplasia occurs when the femoral head becomes separated from the hip joint – this is called subluxation. This could occur as a result of abnormal joint structure or laxity in the muscles and ligaments supporting the joint. This condition can present in pups as young as five months of age or in senior dogs.

<u>Heart Disease</u>

Just like humans, dogs are also at risk of developing abnormal enlargements in their hearts, though that doesn't mean that your pet will not live a normal life. Aging could be a factor of heart diseases in dogs but other issues like heartworms, improper diet and the likes can also lead to having major heart problems. Some of the symptoms include being out of breath, having problems in a hot condition/weather, not as active as before, hypertension, obesity, other illnesses resulting to complications etc. If you think that your dog is showing any signs of slowing down, you might want to consult with your vet so that your dog will have proper assessment and treatment.

Dental Disease

Dental disease affects dogs around two years old and above. Gum disease is a very common and potentially serious health problem that your Labradoodle can face. If you notice that your dog has a stinky breath, it only means that the disease has already progress further. It will eventually lead to tartar buildup; tartar is a bacterium, and as it accumulates it can eventually enter the body through the gums. If you don't give enough attention, dental disease can lead to various heart problems, diabetes, kidney disease, and other serious or potentially fatal problems. The best way to prevent gum diseases is to simply brush their teeth at least once a day or every other day. You can consult your vet about the specific kind of dog toothpaste you can purchase for your Labradoodle, because fluorine (contained in human toothpaste) is toxic for your pet.

Obesity

Your Labradoodle's health can be negatively affected if he/she is overweight. Obesity is not just common among designer dog breeds; it affects other small to large size purebred breeds as well. You should keep your pets as healthy, lean, and in shape as much as possible to help avoid complications like diabetes, heart problems, and joint disease. It's highly recommended that you work with your vet to create an exercise plan that fits your Labradoodle's lifestyle. Active dogs like doodles, needs different amount of sustenance but it's also important not to restrict the amount of food that you're giving to your dog otherwise they may become malnourished.

Preventative Health

Vaccination

It's important to get your Labradoodle a shot even if it seems that he is too small to have one because this is vital to their health. Puppies first get their shots as soon as they leave their moms; vets usually recommend starting vaccines when puppies are already eight to nine weeks old, though sometimes some pups already get a vaccine shot as early as six weeks old.

When puppies get boosters, they get a natural immunity from their moms but it interferes with the shots that you gave to them. The best thing to do is give your puppy a series of shots to make sure he's covered when he needs it.

Labradoodle should be getting boosters every two to four weeks until he's 16 weeks old. As soon as he is finished with puppy shots, give your dog a booster shots once every three years but if your vet recommends annual boosters, follow it and go with that schedule.

Quarantine

After the 6 week vaccination your puppy can socialize in controlled environments (i.e. where other dogs are vaccinated). Once your puppy reaches 10 days after its 16 week vaccination it is now free of quarantine and can travel to the park and on the footpath.

Recommended Vaccination Program for Labradoodles

Puppies

- **6 weeks C3 + C2i:** parvovirus, distemper, hepatitis,
- **12 weeks C7:** hepatitis, distemper, parvovirus
- **16 weeks C5:** Bordetella and Parainfluenza

Adult Dog (Annual booster)

- **12 Months C5:** Rabies, Distemper, Hepatitis, Parvovirus, Parainfluenza, and Bordetella.

- It is important that your Labradoodle gets an annual booster to prevent these potentially fatal diseases.

Signs of Possible Illnesses

- **Sneezing** - does your dog have nose discharge?

- **Dehydration** -does your dog drink less than the usual? It may be a sign that there is something wrong with your dog.

- **Obesity** - is your dog showing signs of obesity? It may be prone to a heart disease, or diabetes. Monitor your dog's weight before it's too late.

- **Elimination** - does your dog regularly urinate and defecate? Always check its litter to make sure that its stool and urine is normal. Contact the vet immediately if there are any signs of bleed and diarrhea.

- **Vomiting** - does your dog vomits and is it showing signs of appetite loss?

- **Coat** - does its coat and skin still feel soft, firm and rejuvenated? If your dog is sick sometimes, it appears physically on its body.

- **Paws/Limbs** - does your dog have trouble walking or is it only dragging its legs? It could be a sign of paralysis.

- **Eyes** - are there any discharge in the eyes?

- **Overall Physique** - does your dog stays active or are there any signs of weakness and deterioration?

Chapter Ten: Care Sheet and Summary

In this chapter, we will give you a quick summary of the major points you need to remember that was discussed in this book. A quick glance can be of help if you are in a hurry or if you simply wanted to review something important. Have fun in taking care of your Labradoodles and keep reading more books like this to increase your knowledge and make you a pro – active pet keeper!

Labradoodles Inside Out!

Origin: Australia

Pedigree: crossbreed of Labrador retriever and Poodle

Breed Size: small/large, toy/designer breed

Body Type and Appearance: These dogs have broad heads, their eyebrows are usually well – defined, have dropped ears that are long, well - set and furry, and they are available in many colors.

Height: Standard Labradoodles are 21 – 23 inches for female and 22 – 24 inches for male; Medium-sized Labradoodles are ideally 17 – 19 inches for female and 19 – 20 inches for male; Miniature Labradoodles are 14 -16 inches for female and male

Weight: Standard Labradoodle weighs about 55 – 60 pounds; Medium Labradoodle weighs about 30 – 40 pounds; Piature - Size Labradoodle weighs about 16 – 25 pounds

Coat Length: 4 – 6 inches of loose curls to straight

Coat Texture: Hair, Wool, Fleece

Color: Apricot, Chalk (white), Black, Caramel, Red, Café, Silver, Chocolate, Cream, Parchment, Gold, Blue

Ears: dropped ears, long

Tail: short to medium-length

Temperament: sociable, friendly, trainable, obedient, joyful

Strangers: friendly, with little barking tendencies when properly trained

Other Dogs: generally goes well with other dogs if properly trained and socialized

Other Pets: friendly with other pets

Training: intelligent and easily trained

Exercise Needs: regular amount of exercise but not excessive because they are athletic dogs.

Health Conditions: maybe prone to hereditary genetic diseases. They are prone to eye problems, hip problems such as Hip Dysplasia, coat problems, and genetic eye problems.

Lifespan: average 12 – 14 years

Labradoodle as Pets

Temperament: very sociable, loves to interact to both humans and other pets, can be quite hard to handle but easily trainable. They are caring, naturally intuitive and loyal pet.

Other pets: friendly with other pets in general, although socialization is ideal especially at a young age.

Major Pros: Has an easy to care coats you won't have any problem in terms of grooming them, and it can help you save on grooming expenses as well. Their coats are easy to brush and it doesn't need regular brushing.

Major Cons: Labradoodles may not be suitable for people living in tight – space apartments because they need lots of exercise and a space to play. Their naturally active and curious attitude can sometimes lead to trouble if they're not properly trained. They don't do well in isolation, can be quite hard to handle.

Legal Requirements and Dog Licensing:

U.S. and U.K.: There are no federal requirements for licensing dogs but it is regulated at the state level. However, you will need to get a special permit if you plan to travel with your dog into or out of the country. Dogs may also be subjected to quarantine.

Other countries: Bring proper documents such as your state permit for your dog, rabies or vaccinations certificate, and current health condition, and other requirements as deemed necessary.

Costs:

Purchase Price: average labradoodle puppies cost $500, sometimes it can cost up to $1,500 - $1,500

Food/Treats: Be prepared to spend a total of $50 for a premium dog food plus food for treats

Grooming Supplies/Professional Service: If you want to take them to a professional groomer you can set aside a budget of approximately $9 to $12.50 or more

Vet Checkup: cost for a vet visit is about $40 or more

Pet Insurance: you should set aside around $2,000

Other Accessories: On average, extra accessories may cause at least $35 or more.

Acquiring Your Labradoodles

Where to Purchase: Private Dog Breeders, Rescue or Adoption, (Selected) Local Pet Shops

Characteristics of a Reputable Breeder:

- Good breeders show their dogs or joins dog competitions
- Good breeders are valuable source of information

- Good breeders know when to let go of their new puppies
- Good breeders will provide good references
- Good breeders know everything about their dog's ancestry
- Good breeders only breed to improve their dog breed
- Good breeders sell their puppies with contracts
- Good breeders offer a reasonable price for their puppies

Characteristics of a Healthy Breed:

- Check the dogs' bodies
- Check their body movements
- Check their weight, height and general physical characteristics

Food for Your Labradoodle

- If you decide to use commercial food for your puppy, you should feed him/her top quality dry puppy food until 4 months. Do not change your pup's diet for at least 4 - 5 days. The puppy may not eat that much especially if he/she just got to its new home.

Recommended Brands of Labradoodle Foods: Canidae Grain Free Pure Dog Food, Acana Regionals Dog Food, American Natural Premium Dog Food

Feeding and Brand Selection:

- Tidbits should only be used as rewards for good behavior in training; the best treat you can give your dog is your company.

- If you feed bones or table scraps, reduce the amount of dry food you give your dog.

- Buy dog foods at small independent pet supply stores because supermarkets, groceries, superstores and the likes sometimes don't carry quality dog foods.

- You should feed your pup three times a day until it is 3 – 3 ½ months old, twice daily until 5 – 6 months old and then once daily after that.

Grooming Your Labradoodle

How to Cut Your Labradoodle's Hair: When you start the grooming technique, make sure to use a Number 10 blade as well as an E – comb. Follow the instructions in Chapter 6 on how to groom your Labroodle's hair on the different parts of its body.

Cutting the Toenails

Make sure to clip your Labradoodle's toenails with dog toenail clippers once every six or eight weeks.

Brushing the Teeth

You have to thoroughly brush your Labradoodles' teeth on a regular basis as this type of breed is prone to dental cavities.

Training Your Labradoodles

Dog Behavior

Dogs must learn by trial and error, they try something – if the outcome is rewarding they are more likely to do it again – if the outcome is unpleasant they are less likely to do it again.

For Puppies: 7 Weeks to 4 Months of Age

During this period your pup should be exposed to as many different non-threatening experiences as possible. You should avoid any punishment that might frighten your puppy.

For Juveniles (3 - 18 Months): You must train your Labradoodle pup to behave calmly inside, and only allow rough play and excitement outside.

Adulthood (18 Months – 2 Years Onwards): Asserting your dominance should really be regarded as teaching your dog good manners. If you need to discipline your pup and make them remember it, you should 'NO,' firmly or simply ignore this "cute puppy tantrums."

Breeding Your Labradoodle

Gestation Period: 63 days

Weaning Period: 8 weeks old

Litter Size: The average litter size of Labradoodle is 8, with a range of 4 to 10 puppies.

Maturity: Labradoodles become mature around 6 to 9 months of age.

Common Diseases and Health Requirements

Common Diseases for Puppies
- Roundworm
- Tapeworm
- Heartworm
- Fleas
- Ticks

Minor Problems:

- Vomiting
- Ear Infection
- Arthritis

Major Problems:

- Hip Dysplasia
- Heart Disease
- Dental Disease
- Obesity

Glossary of Dog Terms

AKC – abbreviation for American Kennel Club; it is the biggest dog registry organization in America

Almond Eye – Refers to an elongated eye shape. It appears as an oblong shape and not roundish or circular

Apple Head – A skull that has a round-shaped

Balance – It is a jargon show term which refers to the dog's movement when standing and/or walking that also projects a harmonious image.

Beard – Refers to the long, and/or thick hair in the underjaw of dogs

Best in Show – A show term that refers to a form of recognition; it is given to the undefeated dog during competitions.

Bitch – A female dog

Bite – It is when the upper and lower teeth of the dog touches as it closes its jaws; it can either be a level bite, undershot bite, scissors, and overshot bite.

Blaze – It is a white stripe that can be found in the center of the face between the dog's eyes

Board – To house, feed, and care for a dog for a fee

Breed – a race of dogs that have a common gene pool or a dog's characterization based on its appearance, function or personality.

Breed Standard – It is a document that describes the official standard from a certain dog registry or organization that specifies the appearance, movement and the dog's behavior.

Buff – It is a white to gold coloring

Clip – A term that refers in cutting the coat for some breeds

Coat – Has two types; an outer coat and an undercoat (or double coat). It refers to the skin or fur of the dog breed

Condition – The condition of a dog in terms of its coat, body appearance, temperament, and overall behavior.

Crate – Similar to a cage or kennel; use to transport dogs and serves as a shelter

Crossbreed (Hybrid) – A dog having a sire and the offspring of two different dog breeds. These types of dog cannot be officially registered in some dog registry because it is not purebred.

Dam (bitch) – The female parent of a dog

Drop Ear – It refers to the kind of ear that folds over and hangs down. It is neither prick nor erect

Dock Tail – A shorten form of tail in dogs. Sometimes owners also surgically cut their dog's tail, making it shorter or docked.

Fancier – A person interested in a particular dog breed.

Feathering – It is the long hair in the dog's tail, legs, body or ears

Groom – Refers to the act of brushing, trimming, or combing the dog's fur or skin making the coat neat in appearance

Heel – A command to dogs which means to stay close by the owner's side

Hip Dysplasia – A condition characterized by the abnormal formation of the hip joint

Inbreeding – The breeding of two closely related dogs of one breed

Kennel – Refers to the dog's enclosure

Litter – Refers to the group of puppies born at the same time

Markings – A pattern or flashes of color on a dog's coat

Mask – The darkish part on the dog's foreface

Mate – The act of sexing a male dog and a female dog to produce puppies

Neuter – To castrate a male dog or spay a female dog or remove their reproductive system to avoid unwanted pregnancies.

Pads – The thick skin at the bottom of a dog's foot or paw.

Parti-Color – A coloration of a dog's coat consisting of two or more definite, well-broken colors; one of the colors must be white

Pedigree – It refers to the record of a dog's genealogy that goes back to its parents, grandparents, and ancestors.

Pied – Refers to a coloration consisting of white patches and another color

Prick Ear – Ear that is carried erect, usually pointed at the tip of the ear

Puppy – A dog under 12 months of age; a newborn dog

Purebred – A dog that came from the same pedigree or breed group

Saddle – Colored markings in the shape of a saddle over the back; colors may vary

Shedding – The natural process whereby old hair falls off the dog's body as it is replaced by new hair growth.

Sire – The dog's father or male parent

Smooth Coat – close – lying short hairs on the dog's skin

Spay – The surgical procedure to remove the reproductive system of a female dog making her incapable of breeding

Trim – To pluck or clip a dog's hair

Undercoat – Located under the longer outer coat; usually soft and silky.

Wean – Refers to a process in which puppies transition from drinking colostrum from their mom's milk to eating dog foods.

Whelping – Happens during the labor of a pregnant bitch

Index

S

T

U

V

W

Photo Credits

Page Photo by user joshborup via Pixabay.com, https://pixabay.com/en/puppy-labradoodle-dog-cute-puppy-2441961/

Page Photo by user joshborup via Pixabay.com, https://pixabay.com/en/labradoodle-lab-dog-puppy-2441859/

Page Photo by user paulbr75 via Pixabay.com, https://pixabay.com/en/labradoodle-mix-breed-dog-animal-1745338/

Page Photo by user litthouse via Pixabay.com, https://pixabay.com/en/puppy-labradoodle-2330324/

Page Photo by user litthouse via Pixabay.com, https://pixabay.com/en/labradoodle-2330320/

Page Photo by user skeeze via Pixabay.com, https://pixabay.com/en/labradoodle-dog-canine-cross-breed-532514/

Page Photo by user litthouse via Pixabay.com, https://pixabay.com/en/windy-wind-puppy-labradoodle-2330325/

Page Photo by user proconsult via Pixabay.com, https://pixabay.com/en/labradoodle-dog-race-pet-dogs-83924/

References

"4 Best Foods to Feed Your Adult and Puppy Labradoodle"
Dogfood.guide
https://dogfood.guide/labradoodle/

"Choosing a Healthy Puppy" WebMD
http://pets.webmd.com/dogs/guide/choosing-healthy-puppy

"Fuel for Fido: The Best Dog Food for Labradoodles"
HerePup.com
https://herepup.com/best-dog-food-for-labradoodles/

"How to Find a Responsible Breeder" HumaneSociety.org
http://www.humanesociety.org/issues/puppy_mills/tips/find
ing_responsible_dog_breeder.html?referrer=https://www.g
oogle.com/

"Labradoodle" Dogtime.com
http://dogtime.com/dog-breed/labradoodle#/slide1

"Labradoodle" Wikipedia.org
https://en.wikipedia.org/wiki/Labradoodle

"Labradoodle" Vetstreet.com
http://www.vetstreet.com/dogs/labradoodle

"Labradoodle" AKC.org
http://www.akc.org/dog-owners/canine-
partners/spotlight/labradoodle/

"Labradoodle" Pets4Homes UK
http://www.pets4homes.co.uk/pets4homes/home.nsf/breedi
nfo/labradoodle

"Labradoodles – Breed Information and Breed Directory"
Labradoodle-dogs
http://labradoodle-dogs.net/

"Labradoodles FAQs" Log Cabin Australian Labradoodles
http://logcabinlabradoodles.com

"Labradoodles – Temperament and Personality"
Petwave.com
http://www.petwave.com/Dogs/Breeds/Labradoodle/Tempe
rament.aspx

"Nutrients Your Dog Needs" ASPCA.org
https://www.aspca.org/pet-care/dog-care/nutrients-your-
    dog-needs

"Pet Care Costs" ASPCA.org
https://www.aspca.org/adopt/pet-care-costs

"Problems with Labradoodles" Nest.com
https://www.pets.nest.com

"Puppy Proofing Your Home" PetEducation.com
http://www.peteducation.com/article.cfm?c=2+2106&aid=3
283

"Puppy Proofing Your Home" Hill's Pet.com
http://www.hillspet.com/dog-care/puppy-proofing-your-
home.html

Feeding Baby
Cynthia Cherry
978-1941070000

Axolotl
Lolly Brown
978-0989658430

Dysautonomia, POTS
Syndrome
Frederick Earlstein
978-0989658485

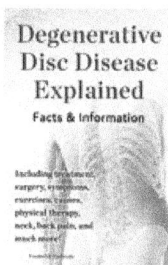

Degenerative Disc
Disease Explained
Frederick Earlstein
978-0989658485

Sinusitis, Hay Fever,
Allergic Rhinitis Explained
Frederick Earlstein
978-1941070024

Wicca
Riley Star
978-1941070130

Zombie Apocalypse
Rex Cutty
978-1941070154

Capybara
Lolly Brown
978-1941070062

Eels As Pets
Lolly Brown
978-1941070167

Scabies and Lice Explained
Frederick Earlstein
978-1941070017

Saltwater Fish As Pets
Lolly Brown
978-0989658461

Torticollis Explained
Frederick Earlstein
978-1941070055

Kennel Cough
Lolly Brown
978-0989658409

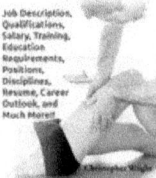

Physiotherapist, Physical
Therapist
Christopher Wright
978-0989658492

Rats, Mice, and Dormice
As Pets
Lolly Brown
978-1941070079

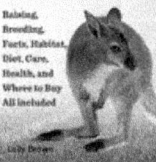

Wallaby and Wallaroo Care
Lolly Brown
978-1941070031

Bodybuilding Supplements
Explained
Jon Shelton
978-1941070239

Demonology
Riley Star
978-19401070314

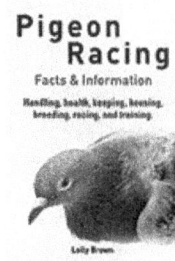

Pigeon Racing
Lolly Brown
978-1941070307

Dwarf Hamster
Lolly Brown
978-1941070390

Cryptozoology
Rex Cutty
978-1941070406

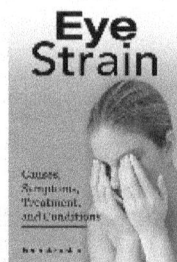

Eye Strain
Frederick Earlstein
978-1941070369

Inez The Miniature Elephant
Asher Ray
978-1941070353

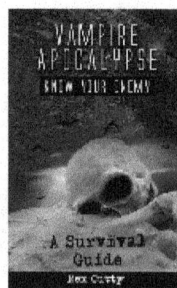

Vampire Apocalypse
Rex Cutty
978-1941070321

www.ingramcontent.com/pod-product-compliance
Lightning Source LLC
Chambersburg PA
CBHW052111090426
42741CB00009B/1771